Dear Noah,
May you leverage
your voice and make
change your choice.
  Kind regards,
  Pam Marmon

SPEAK UP OR STAY STUCK

speak up
OR
stay stuck

Get Your Voice Heard
When Fast and Forced Change
Happens in the Workplace

PAM MARMON

LIONCREST
PUBLISHING

SPEAK UP OR STAY STUCK

Get Your Voice Heard When Fast and Forced
Change Happens in the Workplace

FIRST EDITION

ISBN   978-1-5445-4201-0 *Hardcover*

978-1-5445-4202-7 *Paperback*

978-1-5445-4203-4 *Ebook*

To my mom and dad—

for your bravery and courage

Contents

Introduction

"If you want to build a ship, don't drum up people together to collect wood and don't assign them tasks and work, but rather teach them to yearn for the endless immensity of the sea."

—ANTOINE DE SAINT-EXUPÉRY

Change chose me and that changed everything.

Have you ever felt simultaneously scared and excited? I remember feeling this way at the age of twelve when my family moved to America. We felt scared and excited, full of fears and hopes, yet wrestled with a sense of uncertainty as we had lost our sense of belonging. Our identities were changing. We were becoming something we were not yet in a place that felt unknown. America represented a new culture, a new language, a new way of living, and ultimately, an altered legacy. And yet this change wasn't something I chose for myself. It was chosen for me, and I embraced it because as hard as it was, what awaited on the other side of my fears was my new destiny. Years later, I finally realized that change didn't just happen to me—I was chosen for it. Change became part of my story but most importantly, part of my identity.

Many, many years later, I finished presenting at a workshop about change in the workplace when a brave woman in the audience raised her hand. She asked, "Most of the changes I face in my workplace have been decided by my senior leaders. How do you navigate change when change is happening to you?" Even though most of my work had been directly with senior leaders making changes that impacted people I would never meet, I wanted to cry out and let her know that I saw her. I wanted her to know she is not invisible, and I wanted to validate her pain and frustration. I wanted to help her find her voice, with clarity and conviction, with purpose and confidence. I wanted her to win this battle of sorts—to know she didn't have to feel like she lost before it began.

This book is for every leader who believes there is a better way. It is for the mid-level leader, manager, and influencer who has been told to "go make this organizational change happen" and yet feels voiceless, unrepresented, and stuck. I want to help you find your voice, discover your courage, grow your confidence, reclaim your power, and increase your influence. I want to help you tell your story in a fresh, new way. My perspective is radically different because my mission is to restore organizations to health. I am an optimist with a bold message that we can achieve both profit and purpose with people at the center. I am unapologetic about bringing together people of various levels within an organization for the good of everyone. Are you curious to find out how? I hope my message empowers you to leverage your voice to make organizational change work for you.

STUCK AND FRUSTRATED

Organizational change can be scary because it involves major adjustments to the way a business functions, such as redefining roles and responsibilities, implementing new technologies, adapting to a new organizational culture, redirecting the strategy, or even reworking internal processes. As a leader in your organization, perhaps you've been asked to deliver difficult messages that executive leaders have made without first giving you a chance to have your voice heard. Even though you may not have been included in the decisions, you may have been expected to deliver the results. You feel emotionally exhausted and often find yourself frustrated and irritated at the senior leaders who don't understand how their decisions impact you in a negative way, yet the changes keep piling on you without an end in sight. You feel voiceless, marginalized, and forced to change without the proper tools and mindsets, leaving you postured to fight for survival. You feel frustrated, stuck, confused, resistant, and reluctant to embrace the decisions from senior leadership, all the while wondering if somehow you are sabotaging your own career.

THE ONE THING YOU WILL LEARN

One of the central themes of this book is to: Leverage your voice and make change your choice.

> LEVERAGE YOUR VOICE AND MAKE
> CHANGE YOUR CHOICE.

In Part 1, I address how your view of organizational change impacts your identity and experiences. In Part 2, I explore how the LESS (listen, empower, speak, solve) change management model can help you find your voice and grow your influence among senior leaders, peers, and employees at every level. In Part 3, I discuss how to expand your organizational change capacity and cultivate your personal change resilience.

By reading this book, you will learn to:

1. Identify your new organizational change growth mindsets.
2. Determine appropriate ways to advocate for what you need.
3. Discern what you can control and influence.
4. Enlarge your change capacity.

The greatest paradigm shift of this book is this: You have control over your work. Change is not happening to you; change is happening *for* you.

> YOU HAVE CONTROL OVER YOUR WORK.
> CHANGE IS NOT HAPPENING TO YOU;
> CHANGE IS HAPPENING FOR YOU.

Are you ready to make this your turning point? I know we just met on these few early pages, but I would be honored to be your guide, if you will allow me. I can't promise you that it will be easy. It probably won't be quick either. But if you feel stuck in your workplace and you continue to feel like change happens *to* you, you have three choices: stay stuck, leave, or discover the courage to speak up and grow. If you choose the last option, keep reading.

MY BACKGROUND

My personal and professional fascination with change management emerged early in my career while I worked on an acquisition for a global Fortune 50 high-tech client. What a ride it has been ever since! A decade later, I founded Marmon Consulting, a change management consulting and training firm that offers large-scale organizational change management services and live training and workshops. Over the years, I developed a broad understanding of organizational change as I've led transformational initiatives in the aerospace, technology, bio tech, insurance, healthcare, nonprofit, financial, banking, corporate retail, consumer packaged goods, engineering, manufacturing, academia, and professional services industries. The restorative nature of my work has led me to believe that I have the best job in the world. With much humility and compassion, I consider it my greatest honor to bring healing in the workplace. My first book, *No One's Listening and It's Your Fault*, focused on how senior leaders can get their messages heard during organizational transformations. Whereas my first book was written for senior leaders, this sequel was written from a different perspective; it was written for leaders and team members who experience organizational change.

I strongly believe we must redefine how we view organizational change—no matter how big or small—and examine our attitudes. When we believe that we have control of our responses to organizational change, we build change agility and can adapt to our circumstances with greater ease. I believe that with the proper process, change is not hard. Change is personal, change is emotional, and we are more engaged when we partake in the making of change.

> WHEN WE BELIEVE THAT WE HAVE CONTROL OF OUR RESPONSES TO ORGANIZATIONAL CHANGE, WE BUILD CHANGE AGILITY AND CAN ADAPT TO OUR CIRCUMSTANCES WITH GREATER EASE.

I want to be more honest with you than I am comfortable so I can show you a world that you too can step into. To bring the content to life, I've compiled a collection of stories that represent the intricate journeys of the leaders I've worked with over the years. To protect their identities and maintain confidentiality, I have changed the names and personality characteristics of my clients and have omitted the names of the companies they represent. I am honored to tell their stories as I recall them from my experience, and I hope their stories echo your own. But if their stories fail to represent yours, and if my experience working with exceptional leaders fails to represent yours, could we agree that our various perspectives hold value and deserve recognition? Instead of making an attempt to represent your specific situation, I have decided to let you make that conclusion for yourself based on your unique circumstances. We come from different places, we work in different spaces, and yet we all want to find safety and belonging in our workplaces.

Here we are at the beginning of this book journey. As we move forward, we must agree that others can't respond to our concerns unless we speak up. You are not hopeless. You are not voiceless. You are not helpless. You are wired for purpose, fulfillment, and joy. Let me show you why, but more importantly, let me show you how. To transform, you must accept a new identity, and that is where our journey begins. It's time to turn a new page.

PART 1

The Past

"Change your thoughts and you change your world."

—NORMAN VINCENT PEALE

CHAPTER 1

Your Change Identity: Below the Surface

"People don't resist change; they resist being changed."

—PETER SENGE

I sensed he was mad. Not at me, but I happened to be listening, so I sat with his frustration for a bit. Chas was asked to restructure his department and accommodate a new operating model that his senior leaders were implementing. Normally, this wouldn't bother him, but the decision to change direction came shortly after his department was restructured to accommodate the previously laid-out path, which was now irrelevant. Chas was looking for answers, yet his leaders provided no clear direction. He was fine with whatever the direction was going to be; he just needed the senior leaders to align on the priorities so he didn't spend time working on the wrong tasks. I could tell Chas cared, and I could tell no one was listening. As an organizational change consultant, I knew I could help channel his message to the senior leaders, but I wondered, *Why couldn't he?*

Perhaps you find yourself in a situation similar to Chas's. Perhaps you feel like your workplace has created unnecessary stress in your life, decisions are made on your behalf, and you have limited control. Perhaps you feel stuck, unrepresented, and voiceless. What stories do you tell yourself when workplace change takes you by surprise? Are you flooded by memories of change gone bad? Do you feel overwhelmed by fear, shame, or anger? Most importantly, how have those experiences shaped who you've become?

TIME TO GRIEVE

Many of us experience pain in our lives without properly grieving hurtful, and perhaps even harmful, experiences. If you've been in the workplace long enough, you've likely experienced poorly executed organizational change. As a result, you may have been involved in one or more of the following situations. Have you ever:

- Lost your job without proper explanation or communication?
- Been demoted at work in a way that was shameful?
- Been asked to do a new role without proper training or leadership support?
- Experienced an organizational restructure that brought no clarity on your role or responsibilities?

In the book *The Voice of the Heart*, Dr. Chip Dodd defines hurt as "the emotional and spiritual experience that tells us we are feeling pain." The author goes on to say that "all emotional and spiritual healing comes through relationships. This truth can be an obstacle to healing because the very thing that heals us (relationship) is the thing that previously wounded us." In all the years I've led organizations through change, I've recognized that many senior leaders and managers neglect to offer proper time to grieve past failed change initiatives. I see this often when I interview leaders and ask them to describe what they've learned from the way past changes have been executed in their organization. Sometimes they share ways that change was executed well, but most stories are not of happy past experiences. I aim to capture the essence of their pain and frustration. Story after story, I see mistakes that could have been easily prevented yet had a profound impact on employees. Frequently, frustration arose due to poor communications about the vision for the change, unclear and unmet expectations regarding behaviors and desired results, and rushed decisions that excluded key individuals and teams. Tension developed between departments because of unspoken assumptions, lack of clearly defined roles and responsibilities, and misalignment. Regardless of how the poorly executed changes manifested, the results were the same: frustrated employees, feeling stuck because they perceived that change was happening to them.

Years ago, I was working with a senior leader of a rapidly evolving organization. Change came at the team members at such a fast-moving speed that they were breaking down emotionally. My conversation with one of the mid-level managers, Steve, gave me a sense of the organizational impact. "When I found out about the new organizational change, I went back to my office and, feeling overwhelmed, I just wanted to quit. We grieved for a bit, but now we have put a plan in place. It was traumatic." I could hear the pain in Steve's voice, and I could see it in his body language. What comfort could I offer but to sit with him in that moment in silence and grieve? He was accepting his new circumstance, but it came at a cost. It was a high price for him to pay to continuously transform his department without a moment of rest.

Grieving is a process, yet most of us fail to give it proper time. If you want to move beyond the feeling of being stuck, grieving is necessary because it acknowledges the past, the hurt, and the loss, and then it frees you to accept the future. If you are a busy professional, you may have brushed past your negative experiences with workplace change. You don't need my permission to grieve, but if this nudges you to do so, please pause and take the time to mentally acknowledge what you've experienced. Ask yourself:

- How have my past workplace experiences shaped me into who I am today?
- What am I holding on to that I need to let go of?
- How can I position myself to be part of the solution in the future?

Grieving is necessary, but I caution you not to stay there for too long. If you don't find strength and courage to move forward, your past will remain your present. In an interview, Dr. Gabor Maté, a renowned therapist on trauma, suggested that for us to heal from trauma, we must change the way we see trauma. "Trauma is not what happens to you; it's what happens inside you. Trauma can also be inflicted not by what happens to you, but by what doesn't happen but should happen. When your needs are not met, that can wound as well. If trauma is what happened to you, it will never unhappen. But if trauma is what happened inside you, the wound that you sustained, the meaning you made of it, the way you came to believe certain things about yourself or the world or other people, and if trauma is disconnection from your authentic self, then guess what? Good news. That can be restored at any moment. We don't have to allow [trauma] to define our lives."[1]

> IF WE SEE TRAUMA AS A WOUND THAT
> CAN BE HEALED, WE HOLD THE POWER
> TO LEVERAGE CHANGE IN OUR FAVOR.

TIME TO FORGIVE

"The past is dead to me," said a leader I deeply admire. Her outlook was shocking and compelling. Although she held on to good memories from her past, she chose not to live there but to instead be committed to the present. I often think about her remark. Should the past be dead to me? Am I strong enough to make such a bold statement about my past experiences, or should I carry something forward into my future?

---

1   Skoll.org, "Gabor Mate—Trauma Is Not What Happens to You, It Is What Happens inside You," YouTube video, 1:51, July 22, 2021, https://www.youtube.com/watch?v=nmJOuTAko9g.

The truth is, we can't change the past. It is done. However, we do have decisions to make about the present and our futures. The beauty of transformation is that we all have a chance to change in the process. Is it possible that our leaders from the past have learned from their mistakes? Is it possible that they regret how people experienced the workplace change and made a commitment to do things differently in the future? Is it possible that, like them, you too have learned something about yourself? Perhaps you need to forgive them. Perhaps you need to forgive yourself for how you reacted to changing situations at work—for example, maybe you said something to a colleague that still lingers in your mind. Allow me to share with you exercises that may help with that.

FORGIVENESS EXERCISES

I. **Let it go.** If you are holding tightly to a hurt, a grudge, or a pain, could right now be the time to let it go and forgive your former leaders? If you are ready, do this small gesture with me. Put your hands on your heart, take a deep breath, close your eyes, and say this out loud:

I forgive _____ [fill in the blank with name of leader or yourself] for doing _____ because

I believe better things are in my future.

Although this may feel like a simple exercise, if you do it sincerely, it will transform your outlook on past and future workplace changes. Do it as many times as needed when you find yourself stuck in the past and unable to embrace what's ahead. Living in past hurt and regret is futile. Doing so brings forth no forward momentum. Grieve the hurt, release it, and learn from it.

2. **Adopt a positive outlook.** Close your hand into a fist. Squeeze your fist tightly for a few seconds, take a deep breath, and then release it as you exhale. Repeat the exercise a few times. This simple exercise illustrates a powerful concept. When your hand is closed into a fist, you can't catch anything new. When your hand is open, you can catch something new. In life, assume an open posture to release hurt and welcome change with a positive outlook.

CONTROL WHAT YOU CAN

At some point in your life, you may have come to believe one of these two things: (1) Change happens to me, or (2) I make change happen. Perhaps you find yourself somewhere in between, depending on the situation, but be honest with yourself. Where on the spectrum do you gravitate most of the time?

In the book *Hero on a Mission*, Donald Miller says, "Psychologists have associated an external locus of control with higher levels of anxiety, higher rates of depression, lower wages, and troubled relationships. An internal locus of control, on the other hand, has been shown to correlate with a stronger sense of belonging, less depression, higher wages, and more fulfilling relationships."[2] An external locus of control is when we give away our power to external forces, whereas internal locus of control is when we have agency. Why does this matter? When you view others as more powerful than you, you are giving your power away.

We can agree that some things in life happen to us, such as the family we are born into, where we were raised, our life circumstances, and so forth. On the other hand, some things in life we get to choose, like where we live and where we work. As you consider the entire span of your life, what does your mind naturally gravitate toward? Can you identify ten good choices that you intentionally made in your life that you will never regret because of where they've led you now? Your internal locus of control

2   Miller, *Hero on a Mission*, 20.

empowers you to have ownership of your choices and credit for the outcomes.

To desire control and stability in our lives is normal, yet we all struggle with what is truly in our control. We don't like change because we fear loss of control, but when change happens, few things are truly in our control. Most changes in life we can't control. The sooner we make peace with that, the happier we will be. However, when change happens, you can control your own expectations, your own behavior, and how you perceive the world. Once you embrace the reality of life and acknowledge your feelings, your perspective and attitude changes.

> WISDOM IS NOT TO FIGHT CHANGE
> BUT TO LEVERAGE IT.

We know we don't have ultimate control over everything that happens in our lives, but we recognize that we have perceived control of change, such as having a plan, which typically helps us feel more grounded. Following a process helps us understand what's coming ahead. Checking off lists helps us feel like we are accomplishing tasks that we've set for ourselves. If these things are helpful, then go ahead and insert as many of them as you want into your daily routines. But be cautioned: if we get too rigid in our daily practices, we become inflexible when turbulent changes are upon us.

> HOLD YOUR SENSE OF CONTROL LOOSELY
> SO IT DOESN'T CONTROL YOU INSTEAD.

In her book, *Ask for More*, Alexandra Carter, an award-winning negotiation trainer, encourages people to ask the following question: "What's the worst step I could take?…Freeing ourselves to consider the worst-case scenario often gives us clarity on what might be better."[3] This can help you identify the actions that are within your control and what you need to release because it is out of your control. When it comes to organizational change, considering the worst option can provide you clarity and freedom from fear as you explore your feelings and identify the potential outcomes. If you are struggling with change, show yourself and others compassion while having the courage to identify and explore the emotions that change can bring as you move forward.

YOU HAVE AGENCY

Everything is always changing. Our world is changing. Your organization is changing. Your leaders are changing.

---

3 Carter, *Ask for More*, iii.

You are changing. Can you imagine a world that doesn't change? Something would be wrong. We are continuously on a journey of becoming someone new, and yet our thoughts are commonly stuck in the past. We replay times when things didn't work out in our favor. The most important story is the story you tell yourself. In the book *Hero on a Mission*, Donald Miller says it well: "Very happy people know a secret: a human being has a ridiculous amount of personal agency. A person's reaction to a set of circumstances dramatically affects how their story plays out."

> THE MOST IMPORTANT STORY IS THE
> STORY YOU TELL YOURSELF.

What can you do to find your courage when uncertainty in the workplace is on the horizon? Perhaps it's not change that you are afraid of. Perhaps instead you fear not being given grace as you navigate change. You may fear retaliation, so you hold back engagement. You may fear rejection and humiliation, so you shut off your senses as a way to cope.

> OTHERS CANNOT RESPOND TO YOUR
> CONCERNS UNLESS YOU SPEAK UP.

Fear creates tunnel vision; it increases the heart rate and limits the ability to make sound judgments. The subconscious mind takes over during fear, and we revert to survival behaviors. When you find yourself in that space, pause! Separate yourself from the heat of the moment, take a few deep breaths, and remember that all people who fulfill their purposes in life face fear. That's inevitable and part of being human. It's not the elimination of fear that you need; it's the ability to be afraid of change but make change anyway. You can use fear to your advantage. Fear helps you assess situations, identify dangers, gain wisdom, and prepare for what's ahead. Healthy fear is not resistance to change; it is discernment of what needs to change, and it deserves to be met with a helping attitude, not judgment.

> IT'S NOT THE ELIMINATION OF FEAR THAT
> YOU NEED; IT'S THE ABILITY TO BE AFRAID
> OF CHANGE BUT MAKE CHANGE ANYWAY.

You decide how to experience change in your life by how you frame it in your thoughts. What is the story that replays in your mind? You can't run away from fear—you have to work with it, or it will disable you. Reflect on the feeling of anxiety when change is initiated. What will it feel like to overcome your fears? Why are you afraid in the first place? Fear that you can identify is fear you can endure and overcome. Fear can help you assess your circumstances and prepare.

When we imagine things that haven't happened yet, our minds can't tell the difference between what is real and what is not. If you continually tell yourself that bad things happen to you at work, your brain will believe you and you will notice only negative experiences. Instead, replace negative thoughts with, *I am successful at work!* What if you repeated that sentence to yourself every day, multiple times a day? Just imagine yourself saying this statement throughout your day.

We can acknowledge that fast and forced change has happened in your workplace, and fast and forced change will continue to happen in your workplace. My goal is to teach you how to manage it when it comes your way and prepare you to navigate the difficult conversations that will be required of you as you advocate for yourself and for others. My goal is to help you find your voice and strengthen your message and to give you the best shot at being heard, included, valued, and invited to the appropriate conversations.

GRATITUDE EXERCISE

A posture of gratitude is one way to alter your perspective about your workplace circumstances, such as an organizational change. Gratitude is about appreciating what is rather than focusing on what is not. List ten things you are grateful for in your workplace. This simple exercise is the beginning of your journey to a new perspective and appreciation of workplace change. An attitude of gratitude, especially in challenging workplace moments when you want to be upset, and perhaps rightfully so, will give you a positive outlook and improve your overall experience of change in the workplace.

CHAPTER SUMMARY

In this chapter, you recognized and grieved poorly executed workplace changes that have happened in your life. By forgiving and embracing a new perspective, you are turning your past frustration into your inspiration and motivation. Here is an important chapter recap of how to adopt a more positive change identity, which will help you find your voice during organizational change.

- Acknowledge the impact of workplace change initiatives that did not work out as planned.
- Recognize past failures and hurts and extend grace

to your leaders and to yourself so you can heal and move forward.

- Practice gratitude to change your attitude. A posture of gratitude offers you a perspective that enables you to turn difficult workplace circumstances into growth.

In the next chapter, we'll discuss the lies you've been led to believe when it comes to change in the workplace and what you can do to change that.

TEAM DISCUSSION QUESTIONS

1. What workplace changes have required you to have courage to face them?

2. What can you do today to heal from past workplace trauma?

3. How can you find inner peace with the things you can't control?

4. Reflecting on your list from the gratitude exercise, how many of the things you listed were a result of change that took place in your workplace? How does that change your perspective about change?

CHAPTER 2

Your Mindset: The Lies We Believe

"People who believe they can succeed see opportunities where others see threats."

—MARSHALL GOLDSMITH

Remember Chas from the previous chapter? Do you know why I sat with Chas multiple times and listened to his story? It's because his leaders asked me to. They wanted to know how Chas was doing, what was on his mind, and how to help him. His senior leaders cared. You may be wondering why they needed me, an external consultant, to do that on their behalf. That's a valid question. I don't know why, but sometimes a neutral party can better convey messages without the burden of the organization's political implications. I help leaders hear, and I help influencers and managers speak. As strange as it sounds, sometimes an external change catalyst can speed up the internal communications in an organization.

The point is that your senior leaders likely think about you in the same way that Chas's leaders thought of him. Your leaders likely want to know what's on your mind, to engage you, to inspire you—especially during a fast and forced organizational change. Perhaps they've tried; perhaps they haven't. Could it be possible that they care too? Let's examine your patterns of thought and see if they are serving you well.

LIMITING BELIEFS

What we believe about ourselves will manifest in our lives. If we pause and reflect, each of us will recognize that we have limiting beliefs. Those are the thoughts and ideas that subconsciously drive our behaviors and ultimately direct the outcomes in our lives. Unless you are intentional, recognizing your limiting beliefs and correcting them is challenging. Unaware of our blind spots, we sometimes need a mentor or a coach to point them out to us. Let's explore a few of the limiting beliefs you might be facing during an organizational change.

FEAR: MY LEADERS DON'T CARE ABOUT ME.

I don't know your situation, but if you truly have tangible evidence where this is the case, then you are correct. But I've worked long enough with organizations to share this with you: in the absence of quality communications, we make up the worst possible stories. Have you noticed this as well? If our leaders are slow to share vision or progress, we assume there's no vision and there's no progress. We think they don't understand what needs to be done. We make them out to be terrible people without souls. In most cases, that is not true. I've sat with senior leaders in organizations like yours, and it turns out they are not terrible people, and they are certainly not without souls. They care, and I've seen them fight on your behalf to defend and protect you. Those are the closed-door conversations you may never observe, but I've seen them happen repeatedly and I want you to know, *your leaders care about you.* That message might not get to you or manifest in the way you expect it, but that doesn't mean it's not true. Changing your circumstance requires you to make a mental shift. Can you, going forward, enter an organizational change assuming your senior leaders have your best interest in mind?

WORRY: IF I SPEAK UP, I WILL LOSE MY JOB.

This may be a valid concern if the culture of your organization is toxic or you have limited leadership support. If doing the right thing for the right reason causes you concern for your financial stability, consider where and how you want to invest your time and talent. People work in toxic cultures for complex reasons—the job market can fluctuate, people have insecurities about themselves, and so forth. But if staying stuck is not an option, something has to change.

LACK OF CONFIDENCE: WHAT I THINK DOESN'T MATTER.

You've heard the expression, "I'm just a cog in the wheel." It's a statement of surrender. Many people don't see how their contributions make a difference, so they discount their value in an organization. If you didn't matter that much, would your employer keep you on the payroll? Perhaps a better question to ask is why do you think your employer hired you in the first place? Do you solve a problem? Do you lead a team? Do you generate more revenue? Do you serve customers with a compassionate attitude? In some way, your contributions are making a difference, and that means that you matter. You are important to those around you. When you recognize and accept that truth, others will do so too and express their appreciation.

LIMITED EXPERIENCE: I DON'T HAVE MUCH TO ADD.

Early in my career, I felt like I didn't have much to add. Although it's true I didn't know much about anything at first, my energy and work ethic spoke loud and clear to my senior leaders. We are all on a learning curve of some sort, and we all have something to add. What we contribute is not always in the form of content or knowledge or expertise. Sometimes it's cultural understanding, sometimes it's the depths of relationships, sometimes it's the diversity of thoughts, sometimes it's our contagious enthusiasm for life and our attitude to serve and help. Whatever it may be for you, ask yourself, *What do I bring to my workplace that I may be undervaluing?*

RESIGNATION: EVEN IF I SPEAK UP, IT WON'T MAKE A DIFFERENCE.

You may be right, but you'll never know for sure unless you act. Consider approaching your senior leaders anyway. Sometimes it's your ideas that will shift the experience of others. Or perhaps the key is to pass your ideas to the right person in the organization so that when he or she speaks up, your senior leaders hear your perspective. The voice of one person can be easily ignored, but the voice of the multitude cannot be ignored.

Let me tell you about a woman named Lori, whose senior leader, Joe, attended one of my change management training workshops. I could tell Joe was actively learning when we met, but my interactions with him were brief, so I assumed I didn't influence him much. After all, how much impact could I possibly have on a person after a three-hour workshop? (That was *my* limiting belief!) A couple of weeks later, Lori attended one of my training workshops specifically designed for managers and influencers. I didn't hear much from her until the end, when everyone shared their own takeaways from our time together. Lori spoke up with a tremble in her voice. I will always remember what she said.

"My senior leader attended your training and asked how we can make change happen in our organization. He engaged us! That would have never happened in the past. We are used to being told to do it. Now we are asked to participate in it."

Imagine how Lori felt! Perhaps she felt seen, included, valued, appreciated, empowered. Imagine how you would feel if a subtle change such as this took place in your organization and what a difference it would make in your work and for you personally.

As Brené Brown says so eloquently, "In the absence of connection, there is deep suffering." When you are tempted to resign your will to engage, take a strategic pause. Reflect on your circumstances, and then respond. The strategic pause is key to your success.

BLAME: MY SENIOR LEADERS DON'T KNOW HOW THEIR DECISIONS IMPACT ME.

You are right about this one. They probably don't know the full extent of the change impact specific to you. But they will never know unless someone informs them. There is a direct negative correlation between the position of a senior leader and how much truth he or she hears. People are more cautious, more guarded, and unfortunately, the "truth" that senior leaders hear about what takes place on a day-to-day basis is glossy, shiny, and sometimes plain fake. They don't know how the decisions made impact the people doing the work. Someone must gracefully speak the truth in a timely manner. Good information leads to better decisions and better outcomes.

ENTITLEMENT: I WAS NOT CONSULTED ABOUT THE DECISION.

Healthy, growing organizations don't operate like democracies. Although everyone can participate in the collective well-being of the organization, not everyone can participate in every strategic decision. That would be inefficient and most certainly ineffective. Leaders have the responsibility to facilitate and advocate for their teams and to solicit feedback when appropriate. As a team member, reflect on your ability to support decisions for which you didn't provide input.

REGRET: I DIDN'T SPEAK UP BEFORE, SO I CAN'T SPEAK UP NOW.

When life gives you second chances, take them. Living with regret doesn't change the past, but if you seize the moment and act today, you can change the future. Speak up if given another chance to present your ideas, even if you've changed your perspective, and perhaps this time you can alter the course of the outcome.

In the book *Soundtracks*, the author, Jon Acuff, offers a solution for challenging and overcoming persistent negative thoughts that derail your progress: when a negative thought arises, ask yourself these three questions:

1. **Is it true?** "One of the greatest mistakes you can make in life is assuming all your thoughts are true." Don't believe everything you think. It's simply not all true, and we all benefit from having wise counsel to steer us when our thoughts go astray.

2. **Is it helpful?** "Does it move you forward or keep you stuck? Does it lead to a decision or limit a decision? Does it generate action or apathy?" Don't dwell on thoughts that are not propelling you and your organization forward. Simply let them go.

3. **Is it kind?** "Do you feel better about yourself? Are you encouraged about your life and your opportunities?" Focus your mental energy on generating kind thoughts that empower you.

Complaining about the organizational change gives away your own power. The energy you invest in complaining is wasted because you can't undo the change itself. If you believe that your best in life is ahead of you, you need to take 100 percent responsibility for your life. Focus on the opportunities that will enable you to be successful.

YOUR PERSPECTIVE

When change happens in the workplace, we can choose our outlook. Some organizational changes could be perceived as negative, such as layoffs or transition of key leaders who leave a void in their absence. How could one find those situations as a gift or opportunity? Opportunities could certainly be waiting to unfold with the proper perspective and time. In hindsight, we get clarity and appreciation for our circumstances. Perhaps a layoff offers the opportunity for a more fulfilling job. Perhaps a new senior leader provides interactions that propel your career forward faster. Perhaps a new team gives you insights into new ways of working together. Could a fresh perspective help you see your circumstances differently?

My dear reader, I want to share this important message with you: You are the hero in your story. You decide how you want to live your life. Behave as if you are already that person. Imagine what you would look like. Paint an image of who you want to be, and guard your mind against thoughts that set you back.

For better or worse, your perception is your reality. What you focus on, you feel, you feed, and you grow. What you believe creates your world. Remember that the brain is scanning for evidence to support your beliefs, so that's what you are going to notice. What story are you telling yourself? Is it one that puts you down or one that lifts you up?

YOU CONTROL YOUR DESTINY, SO DON'T
GIVE YOUR POWER TO ANYONE ELSE. TAKE
RESPONSIBILITY FOR YOUR LIFE, AND DON'T BASE
YOUR VALUE ON ANYONE ELSE'S PERSPECTIVE.
AND WHEN YOU DON'T FEEL LIKE BEING A HERO,
BEHAVE LIKE ONE ANYWAY. ONLY THEN WILL YOU
CHANGE YOUR WORLD AND LIVE A FULFILLING
LIFE OF SATISFACTION AND HAPPINESS.

Rather than thinking that change happens to you, you will begin to see that change can enable you to reach your next level on your transformation journey. Allow change to be your teacher.

MINDSET EXERCISE

As we wrap up this chapter, I'd like to leave you with a few questions to reflect on:

- What is your perspective on the changes taking place in your workplace?
- Have you considered every possible challenge, benefit, and likely outcome?
- Have you given permission for your past change experiences to rule over your mindset?
- Have you allowed yourself to lead with fear?

- Sometimes all that is asked of us is to take the next step forward. What is the next step you need to take?

Change will transform your work, your team, your organization. But something is more important to acknowledge: organizational change will transform *you*. How? That's for you to decide.

CHAPTER SUMMARY

In this chapter, we explored the various mindsets that you may have adopted during organizational change and how those beliefs have shaped your experiences. Here is an important chapter recap of how to adjust your mindset, which will help you find your voice during organizational change.

- Acknowledge the impact of your mindset and the lies you may have believed regarding your senior leaders and yourself during organizational change.
- Adopt the positive mindset that change happens for your benefit and there is always something you can learn.
- Practice being the hero of your story by not giving your power away but instead taking responsibility for your life.

In Part 2, we'll look at how to use the LESS (listen, empower, speak, solve) model to thrive during the present workplace change in your organization. Let's start by learning how to become a skilled listener in the next chapter.

TEAM DISCUSSION QUESTIONS

1. What limiting beliefs can you identify in your life?
2. Which of the eight limiting beliefs discussed in this chapter (fear, worry, lack of confidence, limited experience, resignation, blame, entitlement, and regret) resonate most with you and why? Would you add anything else?
3. What expectations of yours were not met in the workplace? How did that make you feel about yourself?
4. Who do you want to become because of the workplace change that you are a part of? How do you want to change your outlook?

PART 2

The Present

"Between stimulus and response there is a space. In that space is our power to choose our response. In our response lies our growth and freedom."

—VIKTOR FRANKL

CHAPTER 3

Listen: The Great Exchange

"Courage is what it takes to stand up and speak; courage is also what it takes to sit down and listen."

—WINSTON CHURCHILL

"No one asked me first," said John, a client of mine, when we spoke about the organizational change in front of him. "Don't people realize I have all these things on my plate, my voice hasn't been heard, and now I have to change?" As John continued to reflect on the herculean task he was asked to complete in order to align to the new organizational strategy, he equated the responsibilities given to him by someone else to the grief he felt in his personal life. John had recently gone through personal loss, so his world was rattled by the significant impact he was experiencing in his professional life too. It was simply unbearable and overwhelmingly too much. John had a choice: he could shut down and quit, or he could pause to face this enormous organizational change and do his best to understand why his leaders had decided to impose a new way of working. After a few minutes, John said to me, "Empathy and clear communications would really help me out. This change restarted my grief clock." My heart went out to John because he was saturated in constant change, but I also felt encouraged to hear him articulate what he needed at that moment.

John was right about the need to be communicated with through empathy and understanding. As human beings, we encounter change in many aspects of our lives. It becomes cumulative, and when change in the workplace is not properly rolled out, we can get lost in the information but miss the communication. Perhaps even more tragically, we miss the human connection that is critical in teams that weather organizational storms.

WHEN CHANGE IN THE WORKPLACE IS NOT PROPERLY ROLLED OUT, WE CAN GET LOST IN THE INFORMATION BUT MISS THE COMMUNICATION.

I asked John what would help him understand the organizational change better, and his answer was clear. "I need to understand how it ties to the organizational strategy. If I understand the why behind the change, I can get behind it and support it."

What a simple yet profound insight! Often, changes come our way without a clear explanation, and we are left connecting the puzzle pieces without knowing the complete picture. We feel lost, confused, frustrated, and sometimes, on the brink of quitting.

Understandably, senior leaders are not required to get input from every team member when they make organizational decisions. Imagine if they did! It would be a disaster. It would take too long, it would be too messy, and frankly, it's not necessary. Senior leaders have the responsibility to make decisions on behalf of their organizations. Such decisions are rightfully theirs, and they carry the responsibility for the outcomes. However, why the decisions were made is rightfully yours to know.

By the time organizational change trickles to managers, the conversation should be about how to make the change successfully—not about whether to make the change. Your input matters, but if you've been expecting to be asked whether the change is right or wrong, you will be disappointed. Instead, refocus your attention on what you can control. Of course, if you believe the organizational change will result in an absolute disaster, send warning signals right away. I have worked with many humble leaders who, after hearing legitimate concerns, have paused change initiatives to reconsider the course of action.

LEAN ON LISTENING

We begin with listening because it's a required first step before formulating and offering valuable perspectives. Another term for listening is gaining understanding. People can't listen until they are ready to hear. Prepare yourself by being curious. When we understand what our leaders intended when they made a decision, we are more likely to properly engage and see it through.

> PEOPLE CAN'T LISTEN UNTIL
> THEY ARE READY TO HEAR.

Being on the receiving end of communications requires active listening. Here are three important messages to listen for.

1. WHY IS THIS CHANGE TAKING PLACE?

The most important piece of information you need to understand is the why driving the organizational change. One can hope your senior leaders articulated it and cast a compelling vision, but if they didn't, you need to probe for the answer. Ask your immediate supervisor, and if he or she doesn't know, politely request to push up the chain of command until you find clarity. Here is an example of language you can use to show your interest, curiosity, and support.

"I am aware of the upcoming change in our organization. Although I feel _____ [insert your choice of expression], I am curious to find out what is driving this decision so I can communicate it to others within my sphere of influence and be helpful. Would you be able to find that out for me?"

2. HOW WILL THIS CHANGE IMPACT ME AND MY TEAM?

The second most important message to listen for during organizational change is how the change will impact you and your team. Early on when the announcements are made, your senior leaders likely won't know precisely how to respond to this question. Be patient because clarity will come. Every organizational change requires risk, and you can be sure your senior leaders are not guaranteed a return on the investment. Some aspects of the change are unknown, and the impact could be uncertain for them as well.

My advice to senior leaders is consistent: tell people as much as possible based on what you know. Some aspects of the change will require confidentiality for a period of time. Don't be discouraged by that; timing will reveal the critical information you need to know. If your leaders shy away from sharing relevant information, frame the question in a way that they will hear it and appreciate it. For example:

"Since we are starting to prepare our teams for the upcoming organizational change, can you help me understand the most useful skills we can acquire within my team to support this effort? I want to be proactive in how I engage with my team members as they help implement this change in our organization."

3. WHAT IS EXPECTED OF ME TO MAKE THIS CHANGE SUCCESSFUL?

The third most important message to listen for during organizational change is what is expected of you and your team so that the change can be successful. You will hear different responses to this question depending on the phase of the change. Initially, you likely will be told to stay informed and do your best to read, respond, and engage with the team leading the change. You may even be asked for input on how to make the change successful! Take every opportunity to show your willingness to learn. As the change becomes clearer, you may be invited to attend training or demo sessions to gain the required skills or to participate in company-wide events where you can learn more information. Proactively demonstrate your team's efforts to get the best possible outcomes. Ask about the key metrics that your senior leaders want to achieve. If you understand what metrics they find important, you can demonstrate your team's contribution to achieve that success measure. If your leaders shy away from sharing key metrics, frame the question in a way that they will hear it and appreciate it. For example:

"Our team wants to be aligned with the expectations our leaders have regarding this workplace change. What key metrics are important to monitor so that we can adjust our resources and dedicate time to support this effort?"

Once the change is rolled out officially in your organization, you will be held accountable to deliver results that are directly tied to the change. So voice your questions and listen to the responses before the change initiative is in full swing.

CHAPTER SUMMARY

In this chapter, we explored how active listening can position you to understand the reason for the workplace change and how you and your team can prepare to achieve the desired results. Here is an important chapter recap of how to become a skilled listener, which will help you find your voice during organizational change.

- Acknowledge that listening is the first step to understanding workplace change initiatives.
- Adopt a posture of curiosity and inquisitiveness, assuming best intentions of your senior leaders.
- Practice patience and build trust as the impact of the workplace change becomes clearer and more tangible with each phase of the initiative.

In the next chapter, we'll explore how you can become an engaged influencer so you can thrive during the present workplace change in your organization.

TEAM DISCUSSION QUESTIONS

1. How can I make active listening my first instinct when I hear of organizational change? What behaviors must I redirect so that I can set aside space to listen better?

2. What information do I need at the beginning stage of the workplace change to prepare myself and others for what's ahead?

3. When information is not made available to me, what are some respectful ways I can let my senior leaders know that I have questions for them?

4. What organizational signals would indicate that my peers in other departments have received adequate information about the workplace change and that we are aligned?

CHAPTER 4

Empower: Expand Your Influence

"Leadership is influence."

—JOHN MAXWELL

Years ago, I was invited to attend a special event hosted by the senior leader of a nonprofit organization. It was an honor, and I quickly presumed we would get an early preview of the organization's strategy and vision since it was December and that's the sort of thing nonprofits do as they prepare to kick off the year. I was so excited to be invited to this casual gathering that I brought a few friends along so they too could see firsthand this senior leader cast his vision. He was quite charismatic and famous at the time, and I awaited his message with anticipation.

You can imagine how surprised I was when the senior leader began talking about raising funds. Was I in the wrong room? What does money have to do with propelling the organization's vision? You are probably chuckling here because you saw it coming, but I was in utter shock. It turned out that the senior leader needed those of us in the room, whom he considered to be influencers, to demonstrate our financial support so that others would follow. This must be a common practice for nonprofits raising capital—I just wasn't used to it. My point is that your influence is currency, perhaps quite literally in some situations. Your senior leaders know it and they rely on your support to successfully lead change. To be precise, your senior leaders can't transform the organization without your support.

When rolling out a large organizational change, senior leaders rely on influencers to take the first step and demonstrate support. You have a choice: you can use your influence to propel the vision forward, or you can use your influence to slow down the progress. Sometimes we do the latter unknowingly. I know I have before, and now I understand I did so because I wasn't ready to commit to the vision.

In this chapter, I will show you how you can leverage your influence to empower yourself, your peers, and those you lead in the organization when fast and forced change happens in your workplace.

SPEED OF CHANGE

With any organizational change, we experience what my peers in the change management discipline call the "change curve." Sometimes, rather than a curve, the change feels like a roller coaster with endless loops, but you get the point. You start unaware of the change, and once you hear the rumors and the official communications, you dip straight down in despair, grasping for answers; you may stay down here for some time. Eventually, you decide to accept the organizational change or to exit. If you decide to accept it, you learn a bit more about it, and that makes you more comfortable with it, which begins to bring you up out of despair. With some time and help, you reach a place of agreement and eventually buy in, where you are back at the top of the curve ready to embrace and commit to the change. This is the essence of the change curve, and if you think about it, you can probably see yourself going through this emotional roller coaster during any personal or professional change that takes place in your life.

I bring the change curve to your attention because of timing and speed of change. When a senior leader introduces a change to the organization, he or she likely has been sitting with the idea of the change for some time. The senior leader likely experienced the initial stages of the change curve and has been riding the roller coaster of emotions for a while by the time the change is communicated to you. What most senior leaders forget or dismiss is that when you first hear of the change, you are at the beginning of your emotional roller-coaster journey. Instead of allowing you to take the time and space to process the change as they did, leaders might inadvertently rush you through your journey.

Allow me to take it a step further. Assuming that the communication about this change was cascaded appropriately within your organization (meaning as a leader, you heard about it before your employees did), you must acknowledge that you might have an early start to acceptance compared to your employees. This is where you can use your influence to apply empathy as others are just beginning to grapple with the many questions at hand.

If possible, give your team members the gift of time and space to process the information. Empowering yourself and others requires you to step into others' shoes and experience the world through other people's points of view.

There is a proper way to introduce people to organizational change, but the ideal scenario exists only in organizations that intentionally prepare for it. What if this is not how your organization does change? Keep reading and I will guide you on what you can do.

CONNECTION TO STRATEGY

In the previous chapter, we explored the importance of knowing why an organizational change is taking place. If the why piece of the puzzle is missing, the other pieces don't show the whole picture. You need to be able to connect to the organizational strategy in order to create internal alignment within the impacted departments. Only then can you achieve the desired buy-in and ownership of the organizational change. If the change feels disassociated from the organizational strategy, you will be uncomfortable and everything will feel out of sync. Ultimately, the change won't be successfully implemented. Inevitably, there will be casualties along the way, and no one wants that to happen.

If the connection to strategy within your organization is missing, as an influencer, you can bring the problem to the attention of your senior leadership team and encourage a conversation to help them strengthen their position. Be the connector that lifts others by empowering your senior leaders with valuable insights. Remind them that they are doing their best and their work is important for your organization. Their reactions might surprise you in a positive way. At the end of the day, all people appreciate kind words of encouragement and a helping hand when needed.

CONNECTION TO PEOPLE

Your influence is powerful. Empowering others means connecting to others by inviting them into the conversation. Consider how this might benefit the people you influence. You could bring them along to company events where they can be exposed to a specific leader for an important discussion, or you could offer training for a skillset that will help your team thrive. You could speak well of others to elevate their positions in the organization and thus give them more visibility during the organizational change. There are many ways to empower others around you. What are some practical ways your team will benefit from being empowered? Who can you

CHAPTER 5

Speak: Find
Your Voice

*"Fate is the hand of cards we've been dealt. Choice is how
we play the hand."*

—DR. MARSHALL GOLDSMITH

Have you ever been in a situation where senior leaders
express their interest in knowing how things are going
but you've hesitated to jump in with your feedback? The
opportunity to speak up was available to you, but instead,
you held on to your thoughts. A friend of mine, Diana,
told me about a similar situation at her work. Her senior
leader was hosting a small group gathering to collect
feedback on how things were going. Prior to the meeting,
Diana's boss approached her and told her to be careful

with what she says. To his surprise, Diana replied that she had no intentions of sharing anything. I asked her why she felt so strongly about this situation, and her response was direct and to the point: "Because I don't trust him. He's never taken interest in my work or my life. What makes him think that I will open up now?"

The prerequisite to finding your voice in an organization is feeling psychologically safe. Why? Because our reputations, feelings, and social status are wrapped up in how we engage with others. Although feeling psychologically safe with our senior leaders is not entirely up to us, it does go both ways. Creating a psychologically safe atmosphere is important for everyone. You can certainly speak your mind, but without proper consideration, the results might be less than desirable for you. In this chapter, I will show you how to position your voice to be heard during fast and forced organizational changes.

OWNING CULTURE

How effective you are as a communicator within your company is greatly impacted by its culture and the events taking place there—in short, its ecosystem. The ecosystem refers to the entirety of both internal and external, visible and invisible factors that drive decisions and behaviors. It includes fears, anticipated opportunities, growth or decline in market demand, competitors, and economic implications out of the control of senior leaders. Understanding the ecosystem matters because you need a holistic perspective as you decide how to approach senior leaders with your message.

Low trust is a symptom of a broken culture. People who trust their leaders openly and respectfully share what is on their minds, but people who are fearful of their work environment often hold back. They may quietly perform their daily tasks with little to no passion or, worse, with a diminished sense of purpose. What a devastating loss!

During one of my culture workshops, I challenged all my clients to see themselves as culture stewards in order to collectively transform the organizational atmosphere. Culture may start at the senior leadership level, but it is reinforced at every level within the organization, down to the frontline employee, newly hired contractor, and recent graduate. Culture is a set of values and behaviors; as the saying goes, "Culture is how we do things around here." Although culture is not always intentionally communicated to us, we can feel it. We experience corporate values, and we sense when something isn't quite right. We are all owners of culture. If you want things to change in your organization, go first. Make the culture better. Be trustworthy, be kind and considerate, become a better leader. Step into your position of power and make a difference in every possible way that you can. Your presence and position carries a responsibility regardless of the size of your sphere of influence.

> IF YOU WANT THINGS TO CHANGE IN
> YOUR ORGANIZATION, GO FIRST.

COMMUNICATION STYLE

To articulate your point of view well, first let's consider your audience—in this case, the communication preferences of your supervisors and senior leaders. Learn how to manage your managers! You can either observe how they communicate or ask directly how they prefer to communicate. Observe their personalities and understand the cultural norms and how people interact with others. This will give you much insight. People communicate via various styles depending on their circumstances. Consider how you communicate with your senior leader, with your coworkers, with professionals outside your network, and with your loved ones. You would agree, we (sometimes subconsciously) tailor our communication styles to align with our environments and the comfort levels we have with the people we are communicating with.

For example, you likely use a professional communication style at your workplace; however, the styles you use still vary. In its simplest form, communication can be divided into two categories: direct and indirect. Consider how you want your communications to be perceived and how you prefer to receive communications. Likely you are consistent; if you prefer communication directly, you probably also prefer to receive direct communication and vice versa. Those around you are the same, but some have different communication preferences than you. Observe and consider: how does your immediate supervisor or senior leader want to be communicated with?

Direct communicators prefer to:

- Communicate facts over feelings.
- Be brief and to the point.
- Present clear and precise information.
- Ask specific questions.

Indirect communicators prefer to:

- Observe what is said as much as what is not said.
- Read between the lines.
- Avoid demands.
- Provide space for a proper response.

Match the communication style of the person you communicate with to increase the likelihood of being heard (unless you communicate through rage, in which case no one is being heard).

ATTITUDES AND TONE

In the book *Humble Inquiry*, Edgar Schein and Peter Schein offer a framework for open communication and more meaningful relationships. The authors suggest that if we approach conversations from a humility standpoint, we can benefit from building stronger relationships. Learning how to ask questions, rather than tell or give orders, requires an entire "attitude that includes listening more deeply to how others respond to our inquiry, responding appropriately, and revealing more of ourselves in the relationship building process."[5]

Asking your leaders questions will draw out their best thinking without them feeling threatened or attached.

5   Schein and Schein, *Humble Inquiry*, 3.

Asking, rather than telling, builds trust. When you ask open-ended questions, you leave room for brainstorming and negotiations. "How might we…" is a positive way to begin asking for engagement from the team. Here are a few examples of open-ended questions to consider:

1. "Tell me about the…" Although this is technically not a question, it's one of my favorite ways to get an open-ended response.
2. "How can I contribute to the…?"
3. "What are ways I can be a better partner to you?"

CONNECT THE DOTS

Knowing what your senior leaders value is also important. Your ability to effectively speak up is correlated to your ability to connect your message to the strategic direction of the organization, to the company culture, to the company values, and to desired organizational outcomes. If you can't make that connection and instead simply speak because you want your opinion to be heard, your message will fall flat, and your reputation might be jeopardized.

COMMUNICATION EXERCISE

As you prepare your thoughts and consider your senior leaders, ask yourself the following questions:

1. What is important to my senior leaders?
2. How can I relay my insights in the context of the organizational values and strategy?
3. What would help my senior leaders hear my message?
4. How can I present my message in a way that will resonate with my senior leaders?
5. When is the most optimal time for my message to be heard and through which communication channel?

TIMING

Many aspects of workplace changes are out of our ability to control, but you can choose to speak your ideas at the proper time. Timing is powerful and has the potential to shift outcomes. The good news is that timing when you speak is in your control!

What is the most optimal timing? In the life cycle of a typical project, several natural pauses may work for you. Most people find out about an organizational change after the decisions have been made. Consider yourself fortunate if your input was requested while the decision is being made. In that case, speak away! Share your thoughts and ideas because that is the most important time to do so.

Other opportunities to speak up are present at milestone intersections. Savvy leaders know the importance of creating bursts of excitement around workplace change, so they position themselves in places where people have the chance to see and hear about the change initiative. Consider attending town halls, lunch-and-learns, system demos, and other engagement activities. Even though you may not have the stage to fully share your opinion, the types of questions you ask during this phase are critical. Senior leaders attend these events expecting to hear from you. One of my clients asked me to guess how many questions he received when he presented important company information at an all-employee event. I immediately said, "Two." He was shocked at my accuracy, but the low engagement didn't surprise me. People miss the opportunity to speak up. Does it surprise you that your senior leaders want to hear from you? They don't want to hear petty complaints. They want to hear your ideas and solutions to problems the organization faces. Seize your moment to contribute to the path forward.

Around the midpoint of the workplace change initiatives,

senior leaders shift their attention to preparing people with the right skills to adopt the organizational change. This is your opportunity to ensure you and your team are prepared. Using an inquisitive tone, engage the change leaders to advocate for your team's success. This could involve requesting additional resources or specific training or asking to stage the change in a particular way to avoid change saturation during critical business cycles, especially if the change is rolled out in phases.

Does your senior leader hold office hours? Many leaders choose to set aside designated time to engage with their teams. If that is an option for you, leverage it to get direct time with your senior leader. Get creative! Invite your senior leader to a group lunch or organize a fun team-building event so you can get to know your peers and leaders. Although sharing complex ideas at these types of fun events is inappropriate, socializing with your leaders will give you a glimpse into their personalities so you can properly engage in the future.

When possible, schedule time with your senior leaders when you presume they are the least stressed out and thus have a greater likelihood of perceiving your input favorably. When speaking, remain calm and pleasant. Do not be rude or arrogant or act as if you deserve an explanation. Maintain the body posture of someone who is confident and curious. When you create psychological safety first, those in your presence will model the desired behaviors.

CONTEXT AND CONTENT

"This senior leader strongly believes in a particular leadership theory. Don't challenge him or he will come undone." This insightful comment was given to me by a senior leader of a senior leader in preparation for an upcoming conversation. Do you think I was going to challenge that leader? No. Why? Because in the context of the situation, nothing I could say or do would convince him otherwise. Challenging his belief would have simply aggravated him. Any attempt to do so on my part would have been a futile effort. Besides, the topic was simply a difference in leadership style—not mission critical—so I moved on. If you find yourself in a situation where there is nothing you can do or say to change the perspective of a senior leader, or anyone for that matter, move on.

ONLY THOSE WHO ARE OPEN TO FEEDBACK, OPEN TO NEW PERSPECTIVES AND IDEAS, OPEN TO RECEIVE FROM OTHERS CAN TRULY HEAR YOU.

Even people who are open to feedback sometimes won't take your ideas right away. Don't let that discourage you from speaking. Find people whom you can share your ideas with, and remember that how you share your ideas matters. And above all, be cautious of harshness in your tone.

Over time, as you learn more about your senior leaders, your communication approach will become more effective. They most likely have aspirations as well as struggles to overcome. It shouldn't surprise you that you have much in common with them; they started their careers somewhere just like you. Perhaps some leaders got an early start in their education. Perhaps some had inspiring role models who encouraged them to achieve and instilled in them a hyper-performance mindset. They may have been surrounded by peers who are high achievers. Maybe they came from wealthy backgrounds or encountered mentors who propelled them. Somewhere along the way, your senior leaders jumped a few steps ahead and got a hand from mentors who opened wider networks for them. Or as a senior leader I met said, "People created a little luck for us and we executed on it." Senior leaders are simply people, just like you, with dreams, struggles, failures, and wins. None of us are sheltered from life's ups and downs.

The reason I bring this up is because you need to understand your senior leaders before you can get your message across. This may require a bit of research. Listen for information about their reputations in the organization. Ask how others have experienced interacting with them. Bottom line, for your voice to be heard, you need to know your audience (your senior leaders) so you can understand what matters to them.

If you want to bring a controversial topic to a senior leader, approach the conversation carefully, probing to understand his or her interest in the topic. If the leader is not interested, your efforts won't be fruitful. If there is genuine interest, proceed by setting the stage by sharing what you've observed, what you've experienced, and how it can be improved. Senior leaders listen to problem solvers, not to continuous complainers. If you want your message to be heard, bring a solution. If your insight is not well received, don't assume you did something wrong. A senior leader could dismiss your message for a million reasons. Perhaps he or she is too busy to hear your message, or perhaps it's not the right timing to receive the feedback. Perhaps the message needs to be delivered by a preferred person through a preferred channel. Do your research. Most importantly, ask yourself, *What do I want to accomplish by delivering this message? Why should my senior leader care? How can I earn trust and preserve everyone's dignity while delivering a tough message?*

> IF YOU WANT YOUR MESSAGE TO BE
> HEARD, BRING A SOLUTION.

To ground you when you communicate, consider these words of wisdom.

- **Manage your emotions.** In the heat of the moment, don't let your emotions hurt others. Be careful about what words you choose. Your words hold power, so use them to uplift and encourage others.
- **Be likable.** Show gratitude and appreciation for the opportunities you have and be genuine in your communications. Your character matters. People who are trusted, open, helpful, and friendly are more likable.
- **Remember, it's not personal.** If you hear a negative response, don't take it personally. There could be various reasons your ideas were not implemented. You don't know all the circumstances.
- **Avoid negative assumptions.** Rather than assuming a worst-case scenario, let your attitude reflect an assumption of good intentions.

BORROWED VOICE

In some circumstances, you may not be the most appropriate person to speak and get your message heard within your organization. If so, no need to take offense. Your organization is simply structured in such a way that requires you to work through others. This situation calls for a borrowed voice.

Every organization has voices that carry more loudly than others. One client I worked with kept an unwritten list of the most powerful voices representing various departments. Whenever the organization faced particular changes, the client summoned the voices of the influencers on her list. Sometimes in harmony, other times not, those voices represented most opinions. Could your voice be one that others seek out? Or do you tend to rest quietly until the voices of the most powerful influencers in your organization resonate within your internal department? Do you trust the borrowed voices, and do they know what and how you think about the workplace changes your organization is facing?

How can you become a voice that represents others in your organization? Some workplaces value seniority, others innovation, speed of execution, relationships, results, precision, and so forth. What does your organization value as part of its established culture? How can you master expertise to become a borrowed voice for others and enlarge your influence? One thing is certain: trust is necessary!

IDEAL COMMUNICATION CHANNEL

Have you ever flipped through TV channels, speeding through those where people are speaking foreign languages you don't speak? We hardly pause on those channels because understanding what is being said is difficult. We usually stop and watch channels with content we understand and are in the mood for—some channels are for news, others for entertainment, others for movies, and so forth. To that point, the channel through which you communicate matters. Some communication channels are informal and serve a specific purpose of camaraderie or team building. Other channels are formal, such as an all-employee town hall or, on the opposite end of the spectrum, a board meeting that is accessible to only a select few. The communication channel you select to share your message with your senior leader influences how much of your content is consumed and in what manner. So choose wisely.

CHAPTER SUMMARY

In this chapter, we explored how you can use your voice, the proper time, and the proper channel to influence your senior leaders regarding organizational changes in the workplace. Here is an important chapter recap of how to improve and leverage your communication skills, which will help you find your voice during organizational change.

- Acknowledge that your organizational culture sets the tone for how you communicate within your workplace.
- Leverage influencers in your organization to channel your message if your senior leaders prefer receiving communication from them.
- Practice communicating with senior leaders through the proper channels, with a relevant message, and during the optimal timing for your messages to be heard.

In the next chapter, we'll explore how to deliver results so you can thrive during the present workplace change in your organization.

TEAM DISCUSSION QUESTIONS

1. What is your preferred communication style?
2. What is your senior leader's preferred communication style?
3. When your organization experiences significant change, what is the optimal channel to share your message for it to be well received?
4. What are some practical ways you can prepare your message to help you get the response you desire?

CHAPTER 6

———

Solve: Get Results with Minimum Friction

"Individual commitment to a group effort—that is what makes a team work, a company work, a society work, a civilization work."

—VINCE LOMBARDI

"Everyone wants to be on a winning team," said an executive to me during a conversation about organizational change. Most of my work with people is about the journey, but the destination matters too. When we are on a winning team or getting the desired results, we feel pride, we feel accomplishment, we feel success. Have you ever been on a losing team? You might have felt defeated, and morale might have plunged. Most of us are familiar with being on a team that has experienced a bit of both. We have some good seasons and some bad seasons, but most days in between are neutral. What would increase the odds of organizational change success?

SOLVE WHAT MATTERS

Lily was a client of mine who exemplified how solving a challenge positioned her for success. Lily's senior leaders presented a vision that was audacious and complex in nature, and they tasked Lily's team to lead the effort. It required a massive organizational shift, training for specific skills and mindsets, a comprehensive communication strategy, and execution throughout the global reach of the company. After months of planning, training, and communicating, Lily boldly led her team of influencers to demonstrate a new way of working. A transformation of this nature can take years, and so, understanding the importance of proper change management, Lily advocated for team engagement and recognition along the way. While I was impressed with how everyone rallied together to make the organizational change a reality, I particularly admired Lily's resilience. Tackling each challenge, Lily and her team delivered what was important to the senior leaders as well as everyone in the organization.

While obtaining the desired results, Lily didn't bring her senior leaders every problem—or every solution, for that matter. She was thoughtful in her approach to demonstrate progress and set realistic expectations, and so can you. If you want your voice to be heard, you must deliver the right results because that is what is top of mind for your senior leaders. Think of results as your microphone. You can yell and scream to get attention, or you can use an amplifier and a microphone to confidently whisper your message to senior leaders.

YOUR RESULTS WILL SPEAK VOLUMES.

What results are most meaningful? If you want to stand out, you must deliver the results your senior leaders want. Help them reach their targets and accomplish their goals. Help them deliver key objectives that align to the organizational strategy. Better yet, let their targets become yours too. Although the organization is not a living organism, it has tendencies that are similar. The organization wants to live, it wants to function properly, it wants to replicate and secure its existence in the future. Find ownership for yourself and demonstrate how your work helps everyone succeed. Find solutions to the biggest challenges your organization is facing.

Here is a glimpse into some of the most important areas of interest to your senior leaders. They want to:

- Maximize profit.
- Achieve strategic objectives.
- Outperform competitors.
- Adapt to changing market demands.
- Minimize expenses.
- Cultivate a healthy organizational culture.
- Establish financial stability of the organization.
- Attract and retain qualified talent.
- Increase customer satisfaction.
- Maintain quality products and services.
- Resolve supply chain challenges.
- Optimize processes.
- Leverage technology.
- Increase innovation, alignment, and overall growth of the organization.

Which areas are elevated to a higher priority depends on your senior leaders. The surest way to hit the mark is to ask them to define their desired outcomes, while you remain empowered to define the processes that will lead you to the solutions for those outcomes. This provides you the motivation that comes from experiencing autonomy to problem solve for the proper target. Senior leaders have a clear view on the few things that matter most to them, so don't be shy to frequently bring those up. Be tactfully repetitive. As one of my mentors said, "I don't let my work speak for itself. I speak for my work."

Great leaders show up for their people, and they aim to inspire their teams to do excellent work so everyone can be successful. They are looking for your willingness to trust them and they hope for your optimistic buy-in. It takes all business levers working harmoniously for an organization to thrive. Everyone has a part to play, including you!

TELL A STORY THROUGH DATA

Senior leaders expect solutions to organizational problems, and data is the most powerful and preferred way senior leaders assess if the organization has achieved the desired results. Most senior leaders are presented with data on a regular basis. The data is most often financial, but it could be in the form of headcount for HR, safety for manufacturing, number of widgets for production, and so forth. Executive senior leaders are interested in various types of data; data is their language. They regularly consume it and they are fluent in it. If you want to tell your senior leader that you and your team are reaching milestones, become comfortable with communicating data. Ask yourself, *What data does my senior leader most often discuss with my team?*

We all can appreciate a good story, the kind that has ups and downs, challenges and opportunities, successes and failures and triumphs. The most effective communicators tell compelling stories that captivate the interest of their audience. To make stories even more powerful, leverage data that adds credibility and validity to your message. Consider the problem you are solving and how the challenge has presented an opportunity to persevere and overcome an obstacle. Use graphs, charts, and visual images that probe beyond the obvious observations and leads the data consumer to greater understanding, which leads to better decision making. If done correctly, a visual element and on-point design can evoke an emotional response. Demonstrate how analysis can be the catalyst to creativity and innovation—how you can transform a fact into an action.

In the book *DataStory*, communication expert Nancy Duarte says that "by transforming your data into vivid scenes and structuring your delivery in the shape of a story, you will make your audience care about what your data says." She goes on to say that "story also has the ability to help the listener embrace how they may need to change, because the message transfers into their heart and mind."[6] Using story as a way to convey data allows for the factual to become emotional, for the objective to become subjective, for the rigid to become memorable.

CHAPTER SUMMARY

In this chapter, we explored how communicating results will catch the attention of your senior leader and position you for success. Here is an important chapter recap of how to use results as you communicate, which will help you find your voice during organizational change.

- Acknowledge that your senior leader has particular interest in a specific set of organizational metrics.
- Leverage data and stories to communicate how you and your team are supporting the organizational strategy and the change in your workplace.
- Practice achieving and communicating metrics that your senior leader values to optimize your messages being heard.

6   Duarte, *DataStory*, 5.

In Part 3, we'll explore how you can prepare yourself and your organization for future change. Let's get started by learning how to expand your personal and organizational change resilience in the next chapter.

TEAM DISCUSSION QUESTIONS

1. What do you know about your senior leader that may help you communicate more effectively?
2. What data, results, or information is important to your senior leader?
3. How can you achieve and communicate the results of the change initiative to support the organizational mission?
4. What organizational problems can you solve pro-actively to provide greater value around the change initiative?

PART 3

The Future

"A smooth sea never made a skilled sailor."

—FRANKLIN D. ROOSEVELT

CHAPTER 7

Becoming Change Resilient: You and Us

"Resilience is not resistance to suffering. It's the capacity to bend without breaking."

—ADAM GRANT

In their book *Managing Change with Personal Resilience*, Linda Hoopes and Mark Kelly define resilience as "the ability to bounce back from setbacks and keep going toward your goal even more effectively than before." The authors continue by stating that resilience is "the capacity to absorb high levels of change and maintain [your] levels of performance. The agility that resilient people show in the face of adversity results from having a certain elasticity that allows them to remain relatively calm in unpredictable environments."[7]

I used to think that the change resilience Hoopes and Kelly refer to was primarily about personal inner strength. I was wrong. Change resilience is about an entire ecosystem that nourishes, challenges, encourages, supports, and then surprises each of us. But here's the hard truth: change resilience is not about you; it's about us, together, because our interdependency and connection is precisely at the heart of resilience. Allow me to explain why.

> CHANGE RESILIENCE IS NOT ABOUT YOU;
> IT'S ABOUT US, TOGETHER, BECAUSE OUR
> INTERDEPENDENCY AND CONNECTION IS
> PRECISELY AT THE HEART OF RESILIENCE.

Change resilience is foundational to your professional success and personal joy, especially when faced with something like fast and forced organizational change. It has transformed my life, and I think you too can enjoy its benefits. The purpose of growing your change resilience is not so that you can push harder, work longer, or fight tougher. The purpose for growing your change resilience is so you can discover strength to uplift you and refuel

---

7   Hoopes and Kelly, *Managing Change with Personal Resilience*, 6, 10.

you, to give you endurance and propel you beyond your perceived limitations.

After years of practicing organizational change and observing countless leaders, I have concluded that one key characteristic of resilient people and resilient organizations is a healthy culture built on trust and mutual respect. What does a healthy culture offer us? A healthy culture offers us safety and connection. With every interaction, we are subconsciously asking ourselves (1) *Am I safe here?* and (2) *Do people care about me?* When we feel psychologically safe within a group of people and we feel like we are known and loved, our capacity for resilience expands. Safety, connection, and a sense of belonging is what others offer us through relationships, and we offer the same to others in exchange. Culture is not the corporate handbook. It is the set of values expressed through interactions with our colleagues. Culture is how we do our work, how we communicate, how we exchange ideas and feedback, and how we support one another. Workplace connections reinforce the organizational values, the acceptable behaviors, the spoken and unspoken rules of engagement, the motivation and inspiration and recognition, the norms, and the value we place on teamwork.

> A HEALTHY CULTURE OFFERS US
> SAFETY AND CONNECTION.

Create a change-resilient organization by nurturing a healthy culture. In my experience as a change management consultant, I have witnessed organizations with exceptionally healthy cultures as well as those that demonstrate extremely unhealthy cultures. Although one could agree that productivity suffers in unhealthy cultures, the human cost is extravagantly unimaginable. The symptoms of unhealthy organizations include lack of trust at the senior leadership level, misaligned departments, lack of communications and thus missed opportunities for engagement, secrecy and blame, shaming, micromanaging, and unproductive employees. Yet the most significant impact of unhealthy cultures is the human cost. When a team is dysfunctional, negativity trickles into the team members' lives outside of work, impacting their families and communities in a negative way. The damage can be devastating. But the good news is that each one of us can do something about it.

> CREATE A CHANGE-RESILIENT ORGANIZATION
> BY NURTURING A HEALTHY CULTURE.

You may be thinking, *But, Pam, I can't change culture!*

I'm just a manager trying to do the right thing, and I am constantly fighting with my peers to get what my team needs. What can I do to make a difference? Don't give your agency away by surrendering! If the culture is toxic and dysfunction is evident in every department, then get out. Certainly, fighting your way through negative cultural norms will get you nowhere. Respect is essential for every working relationship, and if it's lacking, your enjoyment of life will diminish. If your organizational culture is based on trust and respect, then you can set an example by how you lead and collaborate with your team.

In the book *The Culture Code*, author Daniel Coyle defines culture as "a set of living relationships working toward a shared goal." Coyle offers a handful of practical suggestions for achieving highly successful cultures, including to:

- Overcommunicate your listening to ensure connection.
- Spotlight your fallibility to create safety.
- Embrace the messenger to encourage feedback.
- Preview future connection to inspire a vision of the future.
- Overdo thank-yous to affirm the relationships.
- Be painstaking in the hiring process to ensure fit.

- Eliminate bad apples to uproot unwanted behavior.
- Make sure everyone has a voice to encourage inclusion.
- Embrace fun to increase safety and connection.[8]

Everyone has a role in cultivating a healthy culture within organizations. Everyone can show gratitude. Everyone can extend trust. Everyone can display respect. Everyone can contribute positively to a shared vision. Everyone can, and that means you can too.

In this chapter, I want to give you a few ideas for how, apart from collective efforts to build change resilience, you can expand on your own personal resilience to help you with organizational change, specifically in the areas of your mind, body, and soul.

YOUR MIND

The best way to build your mental resilience is to feed your mind new ideas and new challenges and to create new thought patterns. You can rewire your brain by changing how you think. When limiting thoughts come, you can dismiss them or replace them with new, uplifting thoughts that edify you and build you up. You can make

---

8   Coyle, *The Culture Code*, 75–88.

it a game by telling yourself something like, *Caught one! It ain't staying. Next!* Or you can simply acknowledge the limiting thought and move on to a more friendly one. Find a way to identify thinking that no longer suits you and replace it with thoughts that benefit you.

On the other hand, one of the worst things for building resilience is stress. We can't talk about the mind without considering how the brain works. According to an article published by Harvard Health Publishing, chronic stress affects your memory and the brain's overall function. Stress can alter the pathways in your brain, it can cause inflammation, and it can negatively impact your over-all health.[9] When you are stressed, your brain shifts its energy to the part of your brain known as the amygdala. This is your survival center that is responsible for keeping you safe. Although this part of the brain plays a critical role, staying in survival mode for long is not ideal because it consumes much of your energy and puts your other brain functions temporarily on pause. One part of your brain that is disengaged during survival mode is the basal ganglia, which gives you the ability to repeat functions and save energy. The prefrontal cortex also takes a back seat when you are under stress, which is the part of the brain that allows you to do higher-order tasks. It controls

---

9   "Protect Your Brain from Stress," Harvard Business Publishing.

decision making, helps you dream, and drives you toward action, but it requires a significant amount of power to consistently operate.

Even though we can't eliminate stress completely, aim to manage stress through healthy habits that promote growth so that your mind is in a suitable position to be resilient. When we experience stress, we can reframe our mindsets by doing what psychologists call reappraisal, which requires us to look at situations and interpret them differently. In the book *No Hard Feelings*, the authors explain that, psychologically speaking, fear and excitement have the same neurological responses. They state, "The physical experience of stress or anxiety—a faster heartbeat and higher levels of stress hormones—is almost identical to our body's response to excitement."[10] Harvard Business School professor Alison Wood Brooks found that people who take advantage of this similarity by reframing their stress as excitement (e.g., by saying, "I am excited" out loud when they feel stress) perform better. Psychologist William James writes, "The greatest weapon against stress is our ability to choose one thought over another." You have a choice to make by reframing your thoughts to better serve you in your circumstances.

---

10   Fosslien and Duffy, *No Hard Feelings*, 38.

YOUR BODY

Another critical component for overall resilience is taking care of your body. A healthy body is better equipped to handle stress. Consume adequate amounts of liquids by keeping a large water jug at your desk or workstation. Eat regularly and healthily—when your blood glucose drops, so does your resilience. Fatigue rises and your will-power drops. Quality food increases your brain's ability to function. It gives your body the energy to help you achieve your goals, thus increasing your endurance. Take a walk around the office after lunch or, better yet, walk outside if possible. Nature has a way of reenergizing our minds and providing us with renewed perspectives. An increase in oxygen level is good for your brain, good for your heart, and good for your spirit. And when possible, take a deep breath. Doing so calms your nervous system, slows your heart rate, and centers you. Even better, find a resting position and try the 4-7-8 breathing technique recommended by Dr. Andrew Weil:

1. Inhale through your nose for 4 counts.
2. Hold your breath for 7 counts.
3. Exhale through your mouth for 8 counts.
4. Repeat a few times for maximum relaxation.

Doing breathing exercises might seem odd since breathing

is automatic, but breathing intentionally like this is simply good for you and will help your body function better.

YOUR SOUL

As we consider this holistic approach to dealing with organizational change and building your personal resilience, we conclude with strengthening your resilient soul. We are wired for connection, so consider making new friendships and strengthening existing relationships with coworkers and loved ones. As King Solomon says in Proverbs 27:17, "As iron sharpens iron, so a person sharpens his friend." Surround yourself with people who are optimistic and uplift your spirit. I regularly pray and rely on my faith in God for strength, wisdom, guidance, and trust when the future seems uncertain and I'm stepping into unfamiliar experiences. Living in alignment with our values brings peace to our souls. Set a new professional goal and pursue who you are created to be, contributing in the unique way that only you can offer to the world.

REFLECTING ON YOUR PERSONAL RESILIENCE

You are more resilient than you think, and your past can prove it. The next exercise is designed to help you reflect on your resilience and encourage you on your journey.

RESILIENCE EXERCISE

List ten ways you have been resilient in your personal or professional life. Think of situations that took place in your childhood, teenage years, young adulthood, early career stages, and later years through present day. Break down your list by decades, by stages of life, by seasons, by companies you've worked for, by places you've lived—use whatever categories help you generate the most examples of your own resilience over the years.

When you finish the exercise, pause for a moment. Thank yourself for your courage and perseverance. Honor the difficult moments that challenged you yet created opportunities for you to rise and become more resilient. Acknowledge what you've learned by overcoming the hurdles. Think of the people in your life who came alongside you on your journey and carried you when you needed help. Thank them for their resilience too.

After completing this exercise, you will probably recognize that you have overcome much in life. You have a history of past successes and failures that have shaped you into who you are today. Know this, my dear reader: the past does not define your future. With each new day, you hold the power to choose who you become. The question is, who will you choose to be tomorrow? What will you do differently? How can you use your personal resilience when faced with future organizational changes? Once you understand how you contribute to your organization's culture, see whether your example and your influence can help each of your team members contribute positively to the collective culture as well. Together, you can make a big impact on how well organizational change is executed.

> THE PAST DOES NOT DEFINE YOUR FUTURE.
> WITH EACH NEW DAY, YOU HOLD THE
> POWER TO CHOOSE WHO YOU BECOME.

CHAPTER SUMMARY

In this chapter, we explored how growing your organizational and personal change resilience can position you to welcome change and uncertainty in life with a positive mindset. Here is an important chapter recap of how to become more change resilient, which will help you find your voice during organizational change.

- Acknowledge that our collective change resilience is grounded in the strength of an organization's culture, and we all play a part in cultivating healthy organizations.

- Practice reframing negative thoughts and avoiding stress to build a resilient mind.
- Drink plenty of water, eat healthy foods, exercise, and do breathing exercises to build a resilient body.
- Nurture relationships and your spirituality to build a resilient soul.
- Practice reappraising your circumstances to grow your change resilience.

In the next chapter, we'll explore how you can prepare yourself for future change by creating a change resilience blueprint.

TEAM DISCUSSION QUESTIONS

1. Who in your life do you admire as a resilient person and why?
2. On a scale of 1 to 10 (10 being very resilient), how change resilient do you assess yourself today? How resilient would you like to become in one year from today?
3. What helped you cope and build change resilience in your life?
4. What is one way you can build organizational change resilience as a team within your company?

CHAPTER 8

———

Your Resilience Blueprint: Beyond the Horizon

"The time to repair the roof is when the sun is shining."

—JOHN F. KENNEDY

One hot day in July 2021, I walked 10,000 steps with Dr. Marshall Goldsmith. This best-selling author and executive leadership coach needs no introduction because of his immense impact on the world, so you can imagine my reaction when he called me to arrange for a walk that day. He asked to meet me in an hour. I laughed in disbelief and then immediately thought, *I have nothing to wear!* I jumped in my minivan, hoping I had enough gas, because I had no margin of time for any stops along the way. I was in blissful heaven walking side by side with Dr. Goldsmith and gleaning wisdom from him.

It's an understatement to say that I am blessed that our paths crossed, but this walk is not where our story began. A year prior to our walk, I attended a webinar that Dr. Goldsmith presented, during which he graciously extended me an invitation to meet. As we approached the end of our time walking together, Dr. Goldsmith asked me one question: "Why did it take you a year to ask to meet with me?"

Why? There were two reasons:

1. He is *the* Marshall Goldsmith—leadership coach of Fortune 500 CEOs. As you can imagine, I was a bit intimidated!
2. I needed to accomplish my personal victories before I found the courage to do something beyond my comfort zone.

I had to dream it first and then achieve it. I share this story with you to encourage you as you create what I call a resilience blueprint—a personalized document that will help you grow your change resilience and reach to enlarge your identity. Your story will be different and your journey will be unique to you, yet all our stories have something in common. We all have dreams and goals, and we can all celebrate when we achieve something beyond our reach, when we learn, and when we grow.

PREPARE FOR THE JOURNEY

The purpose of a resilience blueprint is to help you become more resilient and agile in the face of unpredictable circumstances, such as organizational change, so that you feel grounded and unwavering. It will reduce the mental, emotional, and physical energy you are investing in wrestling with unexpected changes in life and at work. However, before you begin creating your blueprint, I want to tell you what to expect on your journey.

Your resilience blueprint will help you move from your comfort zone, where you feel safe and in control, into your growth zone, where you achieve your purpose. Although the risk is low in the comfort zone, so is the reward. Take small steps so you can reach your growth zone where you live out your destiny. As the saying goes, "No pain, no gain."

The first step is to move from the comfort zone into

the fear zone. Here, your confidence will be challenged. Embrace failures as your teachers, and celebrate every milestone.

But don't stop there! As we discussed in Chapter 7, your personal resilience affects how well your team adapts to organizational change, so don't find excuses for the things you don't think you can do. Instead, press into the learning zone. Here, you acquire new skills. Stretch beyond your comfort into something new and rewarding.

Finally, just outside the learning zone, right there on the cusp of utter discomfort, tucked at the fingertips of your absolute stretch, is the beautiful, attainable growth zone. This is where you live your purpose, achieve your dreams, set new goals, overcome obstacles, and meet your objectives. The growth zone is where you get to thrive, work like it's play, and play as if you wrote the rules of the game. Play to win because you've persevered and earned the once-out-of-reach reward. This is where I want to meet you, cheer you on, and celebrate with you. Will you come this far? If you are ready, let's plan how to get you there.

CREATING YOUR RESILIENCE BLUEPRINT

A resilience blueprint begins with a daily declaration to inspire you, center you on your vision, and guide you along the path forward. Following the declaration are your thoughts on these eight components:

1. **Daily Declaration:** What encouraging message inspires you
2. **Gratitude:** What you are thankful for
3. **Mindset:** How you want to think about yourself and others
4. **Guiding Principles:** What standards you want to live by
5. **Habits:** What daily rituals you want in your life a
6. **Goals:** What you want to accomplish in the next year
7. **Wisdom:** What you want to learn
8. **Vision:** Who you want to become

Let's briefly unpack each part of the resilience blueprint. After reading each of the following sections, fill in the corresponding section on the blueprint template available later in this chapter (or download the template from marmonconsulting.com). In this way, I will leave you with a personalized resilience blueprint to reflect on as you begin each day.

DAILY DECLARATION

As you prepare for future organizational changes and other unexpected circumstances, you will benefit from a daily reminder of the way you are choosing to live your life. Create a daily declaration for yourself. In the blueprint template, write a few encouraging and motivating sentences. Here is an example of a daily declaration to inspire your process:

I believe my best days are ahead of me. I invest in what's important to me and take risks. Opportunities are chasing me. I do meaningful work, and I live according to my values. I am a relentless learner. I give generously and lead with love. Every day I embrace the wonder of pursuing my dreams.

GRATITUDE

When you begin to count your blessings on a daily basis, gratitude oozes out of your heart and you realize that life is full of joyful micro moments. An attitude of gratitude has the power to change you in a positive and long-lasting way. Consider the people, experiences, and things you are grateful for in your life. Which coworkers are you grateful for? Why are they important to you? How have they helped you through organizational changes in the past? How are they guiding you to become the person you want to become tomorrow? In the blueprint template, write a few sentences about who and what you are grateful for.

MINDSET

Your mindset shapes your behavior, impacts your results, and carves out your influence. The most important voice defining your identity is yours. Let your thoughts uplift you and positively guide you toward your vision. How do you want to think about yourself and others? What beliefs will help you succeed when you are faced with organizational changes? What unhelpful thoughts do you need to eliminate so you can overcome challenges? In the blueprint template, write a few sentences describing the mindset you strive for—phrases you can say to yourself when negative thoughts arise.

GUIDING PRINCIPLES

Our guiding principles are how we live our lives. We live by spoken and unspoken rules. Our principles consistently direct our behaviors to align to our core beliefs, so we live in peace with ourselves and not in tension. What standards do you want to live by? What guiding principles govern your responses to organizational changes?

In the blueprint template, write a few of the principles you wish to live your life by.

HABITS

We go through certain routines in life because they have become habits. Habits are the daily rituals wired in our brains, subconsciously propelling us to act. Habits are formative and they give us momentum, and momentum gives us progress. In the book *Mini Habits*, Stephen Guise shares practical wisdom on how to establish habits in your life to get the results you want to accomplish. He emphasizes that your brain "latches on to any repetition you throw at it," and so he encourages readers to find the willpower to move beyond motivation and into habitual repetition. Be intentional with your habits because they determine your final destination in work and in life. What daily rituals help you build and practice resilience in the workplace? What habits do you need to part ways with? In the blueprint template, write a few sentences describing the habits you will work on forming.

GOALS

Are you a dreamer? When I completed my undergraduate degree, I wrote down a list of lofty dreams and goals for myself. They were completely out of my reach at the time, but I was giddy thinking about them. Fast forward a decade later and I had checked off most of those goals. Although I found satisfaction in accomplishing my goals, I suddenly felt unfocused. I thought, *What now?* I had to learn to dream beyond what I had already dreamed when I felt the prompting that the things God had for me I hadn't even dreamed of yet. I began to seek out bigger dreams, the kind of dreams that hadn't met my limitations yet. I began to dream beyond my capacity, outside my comfort zone, and into the unknown future that I hadn't yet sketched out. When that happened, practical goals followed.

What do you dream about? What do you want to accomplish in the next year to get you closer to your dreams? How will your goals enlarge your identity? Where do you get your inspiration? Are you at a place in your life where you need new dreams? What are the practical goals to help you achieve your dreams? In the blueprint template, write a few new goals for yourself.

WISDOM

If we are wise, we learn from the lessons we experience in life. Mistakes become opportunities to grow.

Wrong turns circle us back toward the right direction. Wisdom and understanding expedite our progress; we rely on them to guide us. What have you learned from past organizational changes and life experiences? What do you want your work to teach you? How will what you learn help you live to your fullest potential in the workplace? In the blueprint template, write a few of the lessons you've learned from past mistakes and hope to learn going forward.

VISION

It's easy to go through life without a vision, and it's scary to drift through life without one. Setting a vision for your life is something that you control, so you might as well make it grand. Your vision needs to go beyond simply existing; it should also encompass why you exist. When crafting your vision, ask yourself, *What is my purpose in life? What is my purpose at my job and how can I fulfill it during organizational changes? Who do I want to become? What inspires me to persevere because its gravitational pull is irresistible to me? What problem in the world do I aspire to solve? What do I want in life and why is it important to me?* In the blueprint template, write a few sentences describing your vision.

Resilience Blueprint

Daily Declaration
What encouraging message inspires you?

Gratitude
What are you thankful for?

Mindset
How do you want to think about yourself and others?

Guiding Principles
What standards do you want to live by?

Habits
What daily rituals do you want in your life?

Goals
What do you want to accomplish in the next year?

Wisdom
What do you want to learn?

Vision
Who do you want to become?

FINAL EXERCISE

Here is one final exercise as we wrap up this book. To learn to speak up—to adopt a positive change identity, to adjust your mindset, to become a skilled listener and influencer, to improve and leverage your communica-

'o so, and to become
ice. To reach your
eling of being
.tching your ability
nat life throws at you—
.ded. To that end, choose
.sks to try at your workplace. As
.plishing your chosen tasks, refer to
Jlueprint regularly to inspire you and to
.. of what you are working toward.

Request to lead a special project at work.

- Take on a new role that is outside your comfort zone.
- Improve your public speaking skills by taking an improv class.
- Negotiate for a salary increase or a promotion at work.
- Sell something to a stranger.
- Request to meet with a leader you admire to learn about his or her career.
- Attend a networking event and interact with people outside your network.
- Teach a course in a college or university.
- Write a book.
- Become a board member of a nonprofit organization in your community.

As you try these activities, I hope you fin[d]
experience some rejection, negotiate on thing[s]
meaningful or perhaps seemingly not that im[portant.]
Whatever you experience, I hope you stretch yo[ur]
fidence and go outside your comfort zone. I hope
remove self-doubt and, without any arrogance, disco[ver]
courage that gives you self-confidence.

I also hope that you use your influence to inspire your
team. Encourage them to try these exercises to reach their
growth zones. Discuss how each of you are continuing
to become resilient. When each member shows up as his
or her best self, the whole team is better able to adapt to
fast and furious workplace change.

Now it's your turn! There are many ways to become a
person who speaks up instead of staying stuck. If you
do something different than I've discussed in this book,
post your favorite mindset or resilience technique on
LinkedIn and tag me @Pam Marmon so I can see it and
learn from you. I am curious to hear what you are up to
and to connect with you.

CHAPTER SUMMARY

In this chapter, you developed your personal change resilience blueprint containing a daily declaration and your thoughts on seven key areas: gratitude, mindset, guiding principles, habits, goals, wisdom, and vision. Here is an important chapter recap of how to create and use your resilience blueprint, which will help you find your voice during organizational change:

- Acknowledge that you need to be intentional about creating your change resilience blueprint.
- Leverage your change resilience blueprint to outline how you'd like your work to be shaped and your legacy accomplished.
- Practice daily declarations to grow your change resilience and inspire you in your personal and professional life.

TEAM DISCUSSION QUESTIONS

1. Of the seven key areas, what did you find easy to articulate and what was more challenging for you?
2. If you were to apply the resilience blueprint to your daily routine, how could it impact your outlook on organizational change? What difference could it make?
3. What is your accountability method to ensure you live up to your future self?

4. What is your biggest takeaway from the content in this book?

Conclusion

"If you are afraid of failing, you won't get very far."

—STEVE JOBS

Donald Miller reminds us that every good story has a hero, a villain, a challenge the hero must overcome, a moment of frustration or desperation, and a triumph. Stories are one of the most powerful ways to convey ideas and inspire action.

When facing organizational change, have you been the hero or the victim or, dare I say, the villain in your own story? Have you been marginalized and made to believe that you are "not enough" in some way, or perhaps "not yet" where you need to be? Have you believed lies that have caused you great harm? What story did you tell yourself when workplace changes failed? What story did you believe?

Pause here just for a moment with me. Close your eyes, take a deep breath, and pause.

This pause has the power to change your life. This pause represents your choice. Do you feel it? This pause is the precious moment you have between when something happens to you and when you respond. In the words of the brilliant communicator Juliet Funt, "My dear reader, you hold the pen that writes your story." Make your story the greatest story ever told.

In our closing time together, let's do one final visualization exercise. Pause and imagine it's December 31 of this year. You are yet again facing another organizational change made by the senior leaders of your company. You have a choice. What will you do? What will you say? Who will you influence and in what way? What will you do well? What will change in your life? What qualities do you recognize in yourself that will help you make this change?

I want to remind you that change is not happening to you. Change is happening for you. Take a deep breath as you choose to receive it, and as you exhale, may you choose to believe it.

My dear reader, thank you for inviting me into your story and for trusting me to guide you on this journey. I hope you found our time delightful, and my heartfelt wish is that you find success as you confidently grow your change resilience and find your voice during organizational change. Keep on growing, adapting, and transforming our world for the better. Our future is in your hands.

Many thanks,

Pam

thoughts on seven key areas: gratitude, vision, mindset, guiding principles, habits, goals, and wisdom. Here is an important chapter recap of how to create and use your resilience blueprint, which will help you find your voice during organizational change:

- Acknowledge that you need to be intentional about creating your change resilience blueprint.
- Leverage your change resilience blueprint to outline how you'd like your life to be shaped.
- Practice daily declarations to grow your change resilience and inspire you in your personal and professional life.

Acknowledgments

I would like to thank the change management colleagues and friends who contributed to the content of this book and helped me articulate my thoughts and ideas through their experiences: Kim Graham, Kevin Hoey, Dave Bogertman, Lori Mitsch, Kathleen Kerr, Laura Bovard, Nsombi Jaja, Danielle Vaughan, Megan Work, Jasmine Kirby, Paul O'Keeffe, Nabil Khalil, and Marisol Ortiz. Your input gave me clarity and direction, and for that I am most grateful.

Much gratitude to my publishing team at Scribe. From editors to copywriters to publishing managers and marketing experts, you make book writing a joy. Special thanks to Ryan Garcia, Emily Gindlesparger, Ami Hendrickson, Kathleen McIntosh, Tracy Hundley, Mariana Acosta, Rebecca Lown, Mark Chait, Hussein Al-Baiaty,

Chas Hoppe, Tucker Max, JeVon McCormick, and many other Scribe members who played a critical role behind the scenes.

To my husband, Sam, and our children, John, Gabriel, and Dominick: You are my world! I wrote this book for you, from a place of deep love and as a way to reflect on all the good that God continues to do in our lives.

To my parents, Ivanka and Dinko, thank you for giving me the best gifts a child could receive: love and the resilience of an immigrant! We ventured into this foreign land together because of your bravery and courage. Rosie and I are forever grateful.

To my clients: Journeying alongside you is an honor and a privilege. I am deeply grateful for your trust and for your decision to take a chance on me. You have been my greatest teachers. We beat the odds together and we've had fun.

Most importantly, to you, my dear reader: You make change happen, and I am honored that we've had this time together. This book would have no meaning without you. Thank you from the bottom of my heart. Be the change catalyst our world needs!

Works Referenced

Acuff, Jon. *Soundtracks: The Surprising Solution to Overthinking.* Grand Rapids: Baker Books, 2021.

Bradberry, Travis, and Jean Greaves. *Emotional Intelligence 2.0.* San Diego: TalentSmart, 2009.

Carter, Alexandra. *Ask for More: 10 Questions to Negotiate Anything.* New York: Simon & Schuster, 2020.

Clear, James. *Atomic Habits: An Easy & Proven Way to Build Good Habits & Break Bad Ones.* New York: Avery, 2018.

Coyle, Daniel. *The Culture Code: The Secrets of Highly Successful Groups.* New York: Bantam Books, 2018.

Davis, Paula. *Beating Burnout at Work: Why Teams Hold the Secret to Well-Being and Resilience.* Philadelphia: Wharton School Press, 2021.

Dodd, Chip. *The Voice of the Heart: A Call to Full Living.* Nashville: Sage Hill Resources, 2014.

Duarte, Nancy. *DataStory: Explain Data and Inspire Action through Story*. Washington, DC: IdeaPress Publishing, 2019.

Eisenkraft, Noah, and Hillary Anger Elfenbein. "The Way You Make Me Feel: Evidence for Individual Differences in Affective Presence." *Psychological Science* 21, no. 4 (2010). https://doi.org/10.1177/0956797610364117.

Fosslien, Liz, and Mollie West Duffy. *No Hard Feelings: The Secret Power of Embracing Emotions at Work*. New York: Portfolio/Penguin, 2019.

Goldsmith, Marshall, and Mark Reiter. *The Earned Life: Lose Regret, Choose Fulfillment*. New York: Currency, 2022.

Guise, Stephen. *Mini Habits: Smaller Habits, Bigger Results*. Las Vegas: Selective Entertainment LLC, 2013.

HBR's 10 Must Reads on Organizational Resilience. Boston: Harvard Business Review Press, 2020.

Holy Bible. Grand Rapids: Zondervan, 2013.

Hoopes, Linda, and Mark Kelly. *Managing Change Personal Resilience: 21 Keys for Bouncing Back and Staying on Top in Turbulent Organizations*. Raleigh: MK Books, 2004.

Miller, Donald. *Hero on a Mission: A Path to a Meaningful Life*. New York: HarperCollins Leadership, 2022.

"Protect Your Brain from Stress." Harvard Business Publishing, February 15, 2021. https://www.health.harvard.edu/mind-and-mood/protect-your-brain-from-stress.

Schein, Edgar H., and Peter A. Schein. *Humble Inquiry: The Gentle Art of Asking instead of Telling*. 2nd ed. Oakland, CA: Berrett-Koehler, 2021.

About the Author

PAM MARMON is the CEO of Marmon Consulting, a change management consulting firm that provides strategy and execution services to help companies transform. From executives at Fortune 100s to influencers at all levels, Pam helps leaders achieve lasting organizational change with minimal disruption.

Pam is the best-selling author of *No One's Listening and It's Your Fault*, a book that equips leaders to get their messages heard during organizational transformations. She is also the creator of the LESS change management framework. Pam and her family live in Franklin, Tennessee, and chase adventures wherever the road takes them.

LESS

LISTEN · EMPOWER · SPEAK · SOLVE

Achieve lasting organizational change faster with minimum disruptions.

Our Team Workshops build on the ideas in this book to help you:

- ≫ Improve your communications about organizational change
- ≫ Increase employee engagement and enthusiasm
- ≫ Decrease anxiety and proactively manage negative reactions
- ≫ Keep spirits high and retain your most valuable employees
- ≫ Get your people on board and speed up change adoption
- ≫ Maximize efficiency and process optimization
- ≫ Achieve your desired outcomes

Learn more at marmonconsulting.com

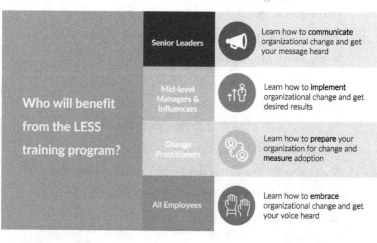

Who will benefit from the LESS training program?

Senior Leaders		Learn how to **communicate** organizational change and get your message heard
Mid-level Managers & Influencers		Learn how to **implement** organizational change and get desired results
Change Practitioners		Learn how to **prepare** your organization for change and **measure** adoption
All Employees		Learn how to **embrace** organizational change and get your voice heard

PAM HARALAKOVA MARMON

no one's listening and it's your fault

GET YOUR MESSAGE
HEARD DURING
ORGANIZATIONAL
TRANSFORMATIONS

🎧 audiobook
available now

PAM HARALAKOVA MARMON

no one's
listening
and it's
your fault

GET YOUR MESSAGE HEARD DURING
ORGANIZATIONAL TRANSFORMATIONS

Leading change at your organization can be a daunting proposition while you face mounting pressure for growth. As a senior leader, what should be an exciting time for your organization becomes a challenge, leading to a fear of change and the belief that change is hard. Pam Marmon shares a refreshing and radical truth: With the proper process, change is not hard.

Discover the practical framework of implementing change to help you get your message heard during organizational transformations. You can confidently build change agility with long-lasting impact to advance innovation, implement transformation, and achieve exponential growth.

Available wherever books, ebooks, and audiobooks are sold.

Connect with Pam Marmon

Visit Pam online at marmonconsulting.com for podcasts, a blog, and more!

Pam is the founder and CEO of Marmon Consulting, a change management consulting and training firm, serving clients globally.

Connect with Pam

 @pammarmon

CPSIA information can be obtained
at www.ICGtesting.com
Printed in the USA
LVHW011112110523
746556LV00003B/63/J